The Complete Guide To Positive Self Talk and Your Self Concept

Danny Davis

Published by Mystic Media Publishing, 2023.

While every precaution has been taken in the preparation of this book, the publisher assumes no responsibility for errors or omissions, or for damages resulting from the use of the information contained herein.

THE COMPLETE GUIDE TO POSITIVE SELF TALK AND YOUR SELF CONCEPT

First edition. March 11, 2023.

Copyright © 2023 Danny Davis.

ISBN: 979-8215009468

Written by Danny Davis.

Also by Danny Davis

The Complete Guide To Positive Self Talk and Your Self Concept

THE COMPLETE GUIDE TO
POSITIVE SELF-TALK
AND YOUR SELF-CONCEPT

DANNY DAVIS

Table of Contents

Introduction

Many of us engage in an ongoing conversation in our minds. This conversation can involve providing ourselves with directions while performing a task, making observations about our surroundings or circumstances, or what is commonly known as self-talk.

Self-talk is the personal story we tell ourselves internally. It is the inner voice that we may not have given much consideration or attention to. However, in reality, our self-talk can have a significant impact on our self-perception and our perception of the world.

While self-talk is personal and unique from individual to individual, it is also a universally shared reality. More than ever, people are interested in looking at the psychology behind their own lived experiences, and this is where the discussion of self-talk comes in.

Understanding the power of self-talk is crucial to conversations about mental health and personal growth. The words we use to communicate with ourselves can either be positive or negative, and research has shown that positive self-talk can have a profound impact on our mental well-being. With this in mind, it is essential to recognize the importance of self-talk and how we can use it to build a healthier self-image and lead a happier, more fulfilling life.

What Is Self-Talk

Everyone talks to themselves, so no, you're not crazy. From the moment you wake up till the moment you fall back asleep, you're actively engaging in an internal dialogue with yourself. You communicate, using your thoughts, your inner voice, and sometimes even the words you say aloud to yourself and others.

You might awaken and tell yourself that you're hungry, that you deserve and need to eat, and therefore you do. Perhaps on the other hand, you awaken and say that you can wait to eat till lunch, that you're not really that hungry, and that you're fine with a cup of coffee.

Internally, we interpret and define our lived experiences. It can be something simple, like how we tell ourselves we would rather write in black ink over blue ink. However, self-talk goes deeper than that.

Just like in your conversations with others, the things we say to ourselves can be positive and/or negative. We can see affirming words displayed in supportive relationships, and on the other end, we can also see clear examples of negativity impacting a person's self-worth, even their self-concept.

If we don't accept the bullying of others, then why do we bully ourselves?

Negative self-talk involves using critical, self-defeating, and pessimistic language that undermines one's self-esteem and self-worth. Negative self-talk can contribute to feelings of inadequacy, self-doubt, and anxiety. Examples of negative self-talk include phrases such as "I'll never be good enough," "I always mess up," or "I'm so stupid."

But how impactful is it?

Research has shown that individuals who engage in positive self-talk tend to have better psychological functioning and emotional resilience than those who engage in negative self-talk. Positive self-talk can help individuals cope with stress, overcome challenges, and improve their overall quality of life.

Moreover, self-talk can also affect our behavior and performance. For example, athletes who use positive self-talk before a competition are more likely to perform better than those who engage in negative self-talk. Similarly, students who use positive self-talk while studying or taking exams tend to have better academic outcomes than those who engage in negative self-talk.

Self-talk can be influenced by a range of factors, including personality traits, past experiences, and current circumstances. Individuals with low self-esteem or a history of trauma or abuse may be more likely to engage in negative self-talk. Additionally, stressful situations, such as a job loss or relationship breakup, can trigger negative self-talk and contribute to feelings of anxiety and depression.

Understanding and managing self-talk is the first step in a journey towards growing and protecting our sense of self, or what is known as our self-concept.

Self-talk can be influenced by a range of factors, including personality traits, past experiences, and current circumstances.

Individuals with low self-esteem or a history of trauma or abuse may be more likely to engage in negative self-talk.

Additionally, stressful situations, such as a job loss or relationship breakup, can trigger negative self-talk and contribute to feelings of anxiety and depression.

Understanding and managing self-talk is the first step in a journey towards growing and protecting our sense of self, or what is known as our self-concept.

What Influences How We Talk to Ourselves

Many factors can influence how we talk to ourselves. Some of the most significant include.

Past Experiences

Our past experiences can shape our beliefs about ourselves and influence our self-talk. Negative experiences can lead to negative self-talk, while positive experiences can promote more positive self-talk.

Social And Cultural Influences

Our social and cultural environments can also shape our beliefs and attitudes about ourselves. For example, if we are surrounded by people who are critical or judgmental, we may internalize these attitudes and engage in more negative self-talk.

Personality Traits

Our personality traits can also influence how we talk to ourselves. For example, people with low self-esteem may engage in more negative self-talk, while people with high self-esteem may have more positive self-talk.

Mental Health Conditions

Mental health conditions such as depression and anxiety can also impact our self-talk. People with depression may engage in more negative self-talk, while people with anxiety may engage in more self-doubt and worry.

Current Life Circumstances

Our current life circumstances can also influence our self-talk. For example, if we are going through a difficult time or facing a challenge, we may engage in more negative self-talk. On the other hand, if we are experiencing success or positive changes in our life, we may engage in more positive self-talk.

Overall, many different factors can influence how we talk to ourselves. By understanding these factors and working to shift our self-talk in a more positive direction, we can improve our self-concept and overall well-being.

The Importance Of How We Talk To Ourselves

Research has shown that the way we talk to ourselves can have a significant impact on our mental health, behavior, and performance.

Here are some authority references that support the importance of self-talk:

● According to a study published in the Journal of Social and Clinical Psychology, positive self-talk can improve self-esteem and reduce symptoms of depression and anxiety (Cohen et al., 2015).

● A meta-analysis of 32 studies found that positive self-talk was associated with better performance and increased persistence in achieving goals (Hatzigeorgiadis et al., 2011).

● Research has shown that negative self-talk can contribute to feelings of low self-worth and self-doubt, which can lead to anxiety and depression (Blatt & Zuroff, 1992).

● A study published in the Journal of Personality and Social Psychology found that individuals who engage in self-compassionate self-talk are more likely to have better mental health outcomes and more positive relationships with others (Neff et al., 2017).

● A meta-analysis of 17 studies found that self-talk interventions can improve performance in a variety of tasks, including sports, academic, and cognitive tasks (Van Raalte et al., 2016).

● Research has shown that the language we use when talking to ourselves can influence our emotions and behavior. For example, using words like "can" and "will" can increase motivation and persistence, while using words like "can't" and "never" can decrease motivation and increase self-doubt (Martin et al., 2016).

The importance of how we talk to ourselves cannot be overstated. Positive self-talk can improve mental health, boost performance, and increase resilience, while negative self-talk can undermine our self-worth and also promotes depression, loss of motivation and anxious feelings.

By understanding the impact of self-talk and learning to use positive and compassionate language, we can improve our mental health, achieve our goals, and lead more fulfilling lives.

The Implications Of Negative Self-Talk

Research has shown that the way we talk to ourselves can have a significant impact on our mental health, behavior, and performance. Here are just some of the ways that negativity can damage our self-concept:

Increased Anxiety

Negative self-talk can create anxiety by inducing a sense of fear and worry in individuals. Negative self-talk can magnify feelings of uncertainty and insecurity, leading to excessive worry and fear about future events.

Individuals who engage in negative self-talk may also perceive normal situations as threatening, leading to a constant state of anxiety. In a study by Segerstrom and Solberg Nes (2007), participants who had a more negative self-view were found to be more anxious than those with a more positive self-view.

Worsened Depression

Negative self-talk can also lead to depression by reducing an individual's self-esteem and creating feelings of hopelessness and worthlessness. Negative self-talk can be a significant source of stress, leading to increased cortisol levels, which can trigger depressive symptoms. When an individual engages in negative self-talk regularly, it can become automatic, and they may no longer realize they are doing it.

This can lead to a negative self-perpetuating cycle where negative self-talk reinforces negative emotions, which, in turn, reinforces negative self-talk. In a study by Blakemore and colleagues (2015), adolescents who engaged in negative self-talk had higher levels of depressive symptoms than those who engaged in positive self-talk.

Reduced Performance

Negative self-talk can reduce performance by inducing a sense of self-doubt and reducing confidence. When an individual engages in negative self-talk, they may question their abilities and feel uncertain about their performance.

This can lead to a lack of confidence, which can affect their ability to perform effectively. In a study by Woodman and colleagues (2009), golfers who engaged in negative self-talk were found to have reduced confidence and lower performance than those who engaged in positive self-talk.

Negative self-talk can also lead to increased anxiety and stress, which can impair performance. When individuals engage in negative self-talk, they may magnify the importance of the task at hand, leading to excessive worry and stress.

This can lead to impaired decision-making and reduced performance. In a study by Mullen and Hardy (2000), participants who engaged in negative self-talk during a cognitive task showed impaired decision-making compared to those who engaged in positive self-talk.

Finally, negative self-talk can also create self-fulfilling prophecies, where an individual's negative thoughts become a reality. When individuals engage in negative self-talk, they may create self-limiting beliefs that prevent them from performing to their full potential.

This can lead to a self-fulfilling prophecy where their negative thoughts become a reality. In a study by Nieuwenhuys and colleagues (2018), participants who engaged in negative self-talk before a cycling task had reduced performance compared to those who engaged in positive self-talk.

Lowered Self Worth

When individuals engage in negative self-talk, they may focus on their flaws and mistakes, leading to a negative self-image. This can lead to a vicious cycle where individuals believe that they are not good enough, which can further reinforce negative self-talk.

In a study by Leary and colleagues (1995), participants who engaged in negative self-talk had lower self-esteem and higher levels of depression and anxiety than those who engaged in positive self-talk.

Negative Relationships

We can also see that individuals engaging in negative self-talk may be overly critical and judgmental of themselves. This can lead to a lack of self-compassion, where individuals are unable to show themselves kindness and understanding.

This lack of self-compassion can further erode self-worth and lead to one feeling unworthiness. In a study by Neff (2003), participants who engaged in self-compassion had higher levels of self-worth and lower levels of anxiety and depression.

Decreased Physical Health

The stress response activated by negative self-talk can contribute to the development of conditions such as heart disease, high blood pressure, and diabetes. Chronic stress can also exacerbate existing health conditions, making it harder to manage symptoms and leading to a decline in overall health.

In a study by Cohen and colleagues (2012), participants who engaged in negative self-talk had a higher risk of developing chronic illnesses than those who did not engage in negative self-talk.

4 Categories Of Negative-Talk

To incorporate positive self-talk into your life, it is important to first recognize how often and what type of negative thinking or self-talk you engage in. Once you have this understanding, you can start working on retraining your thoughts.

Negative self-talk typically falls into one of four categories: personalizing, polarizing, magnifying, and catastrophizing. You may identify with one or multiple categories. By categorizing your thoughts in this way, you can begin to replace them with more positive thoughts.

However, this process takes time and practice. It is essential to pay close attention to your self-talk and identify areas that require improvement. Changing your self-talk for the better won't happen overnight, but with dedication and effort, you can make significant progress.

Personalizing

- Blaming yourself for something that is not entirely your fault, such as a project at work that didn't go as planned.

- Believing that you are the reason someone is unhappy or angry, even if there are other factors at play.

- Thinking that your mistakes are always your fault, even when others are involved.

- Feeling guilty for taking time for yourself or setting boundaries, because you think it will upset others.

- Assuming that people are judging you negatively, even if there is no evidence to support this belief.

Polarizing

- "I either have to be perfect or I'm a failure."
- "If I'm not the best, then there's no point in even trying."
- "Everything in my life is either amazing or terrible."
- "I can only be happy if everything in my life is going perfectly."
- "If I make one mistake, I'm a complete failure."

Magnifying

- "I always mess things up"
- "Nothing ever goes right for me"
- "I can't do anything right"
- "Everyone else is doing so much better than me"
- "This is a disaster"

Catastrophizing

- "I failed that exam, my academic career is over."

- "I made a mistake in my presentation, now my colleagues will never trust me again."

- "I had an argument with my partner, our relationship is doomed."

- "I didn't get the job I applied for, I'll never be able to find work again."

- "I got a negative comment on my social media post, everyone hates me."

The Benefits Of Positive Self-Talk

Positive self-talk can have benefits in many areas of our lives, including our mental health, relationships, and performance. Here are some examples:

Improved Mental health

Positive self-talk can have a major influence over mental health. Research has shown that positive self-talk can improve self-esteem, reduce symptoms of anxiety and depression, and promote feelings of resilience and hope in the face of adversity (Cohen et al., 2015; Tugade & Fredrickson, 2007).

One way that positive self-talk benefits our mental health is by boosting self-esteem. When we use positive and affirming language to talk to ourselves, we are reinforcing positive beliefs about ourselves and our abilities. This can result in increasing feelings of self-worth and confidence, which can have a ripple effect on our mental health.

Positive self-talk can also reduce symptoms of anxiety and depression. Negative self-talk can lead to feelings of hopelessness and despair, while positive self-talk can promote feelings of optimism and hope (Cohen et al., 2015). By focusing on our strengths and capabilities, we can reduce feelings of anxiety and depression and increase our ability to cope with challenging situations.

Focusing on positive self-talk can lead to increased feelings of hope and motivation, even in difficult circumstances (Tugade & Fredrickson, 2007).

Stronger Relationships

Positive self-talk can also benefit our relationships with others. Research has shown that when we are kind and compassionate to ourselves, we are more likely to show kindness and compassion to others (Neff et al., 2017).

One way that positive self-talk benefits our relationships is by improving our self-image. When we use positive language to talk to ourselves, we are reinforcing positive beliefs about ourselves and our abilities. This can lead to increased feelings of self-worth and confidence, which can have a positive impact on our interactions with others. When we feel good about ourselves, we are more likely to treat others with kindness and respect.

Positive self-talk can also improve our ability to empathize with others. When we are kind and compassionate to ourselves, we are more likely to extend those qualities to others. This can lead to more positive interactions and deeper connections with others.

Heightened Performance

Positive self-talk can also benefit our performance in various domains, including work, sports, and cognitive tasks. Research has shown that positive self-talk can increase motivation, persistence, and confidence, which can lead to better outcomes (Van Raalte et al., 2016).

In the workplace, positive self-talk can lead to increased productivity and job satisfaction. When we use positive language to talk to ourselves about our work, we are more likely to feel motivated and engaged in our tasks. This can lead to better performance and greater satisfaction with our work (Luthans et al., 2015).

In sports, positive self-talk can improve athletic performance. When athletes use positive and motivational language to talk to themselves, they are more likely to feel confident and focused during competition. This can lead to better outcomes and improved performance (Hatzigeorgiadis et al., 2011).

When we use positive and affirming language to talk to ourselves about our abilities, we are more likely to feel confident and capable in our cognitive tasks. This can lead to better performance on tasks such as problem-solving, decision-making, and memory (Jain et al., 2018).

Better Physical Health

Positive self-talk can also benefit our physical health. Research has shown that positive self-talk can lead to better health outcomes, including improved immune function, reduced stress, and better overall well-being (Creswell et al., 2015; Petersen et al., 2018).

One way that positive self-talk benefits our health is by reducing stress. Negative self-talk can contribute to feelings of anxiety and stress, which can harm our physical health. By using positive language to talk to ourselves, we can reduce feelings of stress and promote relaxation and calmness.

Positive self-talk can also improve immune function. When we are optimistic in our self-talk, we are more likely to experience positive emotions, which can have a beneficial effect on our immune system. Studies have found that positive emotions can lead to increased immune function and better health outcomes (Creswell et al., 2015).

Positive self-talk can promote overall well-being, leading to increased feelings of happiness and life satisfaction, which can have a positive impact on our physical health.

Enhanced Creativity

Positive self-talk can also benefit our creativity. Research has shown that positive self-talk can increase our willingness to take risks, try new things, and think outside the box, which can lead to more creative ideas and solutions (Woodward et al., 2020).

When we use positive language to talk to ourselves about our creativity and abilities, we are more likely to feel confident and empowered to express ourselves in new and unique ways. This can lead to increased creativity and innovation, as we are more willing to take risks and explore new ideas.

Positive self-talk can also help us overcome creative blocks and challenges. When we use positive language to talk to ourselves about our ability to overcome obstacles, we are more likely to persevere in the face of adversity and find creative solutions to problems. This can help us break through creative blocks and push ourselves to new levels of creativity.

When we use positive language to talk to ourselves about our creative goals and aspirations, we are more likely to feel motivated and inspired to pursue our passions. This can lead to a deeper sense of fulfillment and satisfaction in our creative endeavors.

What Is Self-Concept

Self-concept refers to the collection of beliefs, attitudes, and perceptions that individuals have about themselves. It is the way we see ourselves, and it includes our thoughts and feelings about our abilities, personality, values, and roles. Self-concept is a fundamental aspect of human psychology, and it plays a vital role in our mental health, interpersonal relationships, and overall well-being.

The development of self-concept begins in childhood and continues throughout our lives, shaped by our experiences, interactions, and feedback from others. As we grow and mature, we form a self-concept that is unique to us, based on our perceptions of ourselves and our place in the world. Our self-concept influences how we behave, how we interpret the world around us, and how we relate to others.

According to social identity theory, self-concept is composed of two main components: personal identity and social identity. Personal identity refers to our characteristics, such as our personality traits, values, and abilities.

Social identity, on the other hand, refers to the groups or categories to which we belong, such as our gender, race, ethnicity, religion, or profession. Our social identity can have a significant impact on our self-concept, as it shapes our sense of belonging and connection to others.

Research has shown that self-concept is closely linked to mental health and well-being. A positive self-concept, characterized by high self-esteem, self-worth, and self-efficacy, is associated with better psychological functioning, including lower levels of depression, anxiety, and stress.

Conversely, a negative self-concept, marked by low self-esteem, self-doubt, and self-criticism, can lead to a range of mental health problems, such as mood disorders and eating disorders.

Moreover, self-concept can affect our interpersonal relationships, as it influences how we communicate, express ourselves, and interact with others. Individuals with a positive self-concept tend to have healthier and more satisfying relationships, as they are more confident, assertive, and empathetic. On the other hand, those with a negative self-concept may struggle in relationships, as they may be insecure, avoidant, or dependent on others for validation.

Several factors can influence the development of self-concept, including cultural, social, and environmental factors. For example, cultural values and beliefs can shape our self-concept by influencing our sense of identity and belonging.

Socialization processes, such as family dynamics and peer relationships, can also have a significant impact on self-concept formation. Additionally, environmental factors, such as socioeconomic status and access to resources, can affect our self-concept by influencing our opportunities and experiences.

Self-concept is a complex and multifaceted construct that plays a vital role in our mental health, interpersonal relationships, and overall well-being. It is shaped by a range of factors, including individual characteristics, social identity, cultural values, and environmental factors.

A positive self-concept is associated with better psychological functioning and healthier relationships, while a negative self-concept can lead to a range of mental health problems and interpersonal difficulties.

Understanding and cultivating a healthy self-concept is essential for personal growth, resilience, and fulfillment.

6 Daily Habits To Elevate Your Self-Concept

Here are some daily habits that can elevate our self-concept:

Practice Self-Compassion

Practicing self-compassion involves treating oneself with kindness, understanding, and acceptance, particularly in times of difficulty or failure. Research has shown that self-compassion is associated with numerous positive outcomes, including improved mental health, greater life satisfaction, and better relationships. Additionally, practicing self-compassion has been linked to a more positive self-concept.

Self-compassion helps individuals develop a more realistic and positive view of themselves by reducing self-criticism and self-judgment. Instead of being overly critical of themselves for their mistakes or failures, individuals who practice self-compassion can acknowledge their shortcomings with kindness and understanding. This can lead to a more compassionate and accepting attitude toward oneself, which can contribute to a more positive self-concept.

One study found that self-compassion was positively associated with self-esteem, self-efficacy, and subjective well-being, and negatively associated with depression, anxiety, and stress (Neff & McGehee, 2010).

Another study found that self-compassion was associated with a more positive body image, even among individuals with body dissatisfaction (Wasylkiw, MacKinnon, & MacLellan, 2012).

Practicing self-compassion can also help individuals cope with setbacks and challenges, which can contribute to a more positive self-concept. One study found that individuals who practiced self-compassion were better able to cope with a stressful life event and had more positive views of themselves following the event (Leary et al., 2007).

Practicing self-compassion can benefit one's self-concept by reducing self-criticism and judgment, increasing self-acceptance and self-compassion, and improving one's ability to cope with setbacks and challenges. These benefits can contribute to a more positive and resilient self-concept, which can lead to greater happiness, well-being, and success in various domains of life.

Set Achievable Goals

Setting achievable goals is an effective way to elevate our self-concept. When we set goals that are within our reach, we are more likely to achieve them, which can boost our confidence and self-esteem. In addition, setting achievable goals helps us to focus our efforts and make progress toward the things we want to accomplish.

Research has shown that setting achievable goals is an important component of success in a variety of areas, including academic achievement, sports performance, and job performance. A study published in the Journal of Applied Psychology found that goal setting was positively related to job performance, especially when goals were specific and challenging, but still achievable (Locke & Latham, 2002).

Another study found that goal-setting was positively related to academic achievement, especially when goals were moderately difficult and feedback was provided on progress toward those goals (Zimmerman & Kitsantas, 1997).

Setting achievable goals can also help us to develop a more positive self-concept by giving us a sense of control over our lives. When we set goals, we are actively working toward something that we want to achieve, which can give us a sense of purpose and direction. Additionally, achieving our goals can reinforce our belief in our abilities and potential.

However, it's important to note that setting goals that are too challenging or unrealistic can have the opposite effect on our self-concept. When we set goals that are too difficult or unattainable, we may feel discouraged or defeated when we are unable to achieve them. This can lead to negative self-talk and a decrease in self-esteem.

Therefore, it's important to set goals that are challenging but still achievable.

Focus On Your Strengths

What are your strengths? Focusing on them is an effective way to elevate our self-concept. When we focus on our strengths, we are more likely to feel confident, capable, and positive about ourselves. In addition, focusing on our strengths can help us to identify areas where we excel, which can lead to greater success and fulfillment in various areas of our lives.

Research has shown that focusing on our strengths can have a positive impact on our self-concept. A study published in the Journal of Positive Psychology found that focusing on one's strengths was associated with greater happiness and life satisfaction (Govindji & Linley, 2007). Another study found that focusing on one's strengths was associated with better performance in academic and work settings (Linley, Nielsen, Gillett, & Biswas-Diener, 2010).

Focusing on our strengths can also help us to develop a more positive self-concept by shifting our focus away from our weaknesses and limitations. When we focus on our weaknesses, we may feel inadequate or discouraged, which can lead to negative self-talk and a decrease in self-esteem. However, when we focus on our strengths, we are more likely to feel optimistic about ourselves.

It's important to note that focusing on our strengths does not mean ignoring our weaknesses or areas where we need to improve. Rather, it means recognizing our strengths and using them to overcome our weaknesses and achieve our goals. By focusing on our strengths, we can develop a more balanced and realistic view of ourselves, which can contribute to greater confidence and resilience.

By recognizing and utilizing our strengths, we can develop a more positive and balanced self-concept, which can contribute to greater happiness and success in various areas of our lives.

Surround Yourself With Positive People

Surrounding yourself with the right people can have a significant impact on your self-concept. Our social environment plays a critical role in shaping how we see ourselves, our beliefs, and our behaviors. Being around positive, supportive, and encouraging people can boost our self-esteem, increase our confidence, and elevate our self-concept. On the other hand, being around negative, critical, or unsupportive people can undermine our self-esteem, decrease our confidence, and lower our self-concept.

Research has shown that social support can have a positive impact on our self-concept. A study published in the Journal of Personality and Social Psychology found that having a supportive social network was associated with greater self-esteem (Heatherton & Polivy, 1991). Another study found that social support was a significant predictor of positive self-concept among adolescents (Vida & Cramer, 2016).

Surrounding yourself with the right people can also help you to develop more positive and realistic beliefs about yourself. When we are around people who believe in us, appreciate our strengths, and provide positive feedback, we are more likely to see ourselves in a positive light. This, in turn, can lead to increased confidence, motivation, and a more optimistic outlook on life.

It's important to note that surrounding yourself with the right people doesn't mean surrounding yourself with people who always agree with you or never challenge you. Rather, it means surrounding yourself with people who respect you, supports you, and help you grow. These people may challenge you, provide constructive feedback, and help you develop new skills and perspectives, but they do so positively and encouragingly.

Get the right people in your corner. By choosing to surround yourself with positive and supportive people, you can create a social environment that nurtures and enhances your sense of self-worth and confidence.

Practice Gratitude

Practicing gratitude can have a significant impact on our self-concept. Gratitude is the act of acknowledging and appreciating the good things in our lives, both big and small. When we focus on what we are grateful for, we cultivate a positive mindset and increase our sense of well-being. This, in turn, can lead to a more positive self-concept.

Research has shown that practicing gratitude can increase our self-esteem and self-worth. A study published in the Journal of Applied Sport Psychology found that athletes who practiced gratitude had higher self-esteem than those who did not (Bono et al., 2010).

Another study found that participants who wrote letters of gratitude experienced an increase in self-worth and decreased symptoms of depression (Toepfer et al., 2012).

Practicing gratitude can also help us to see ourselves in a more positive light. When we focus on what we are grateful for, we shift our attention away from negative thoughts and emotions and focus on the positive aspects of our lives. This can lead to increased feelings of self-acceptance, self-love, and self-compassion.

There are many ways to practice gratitude, such as keeping a gratitude journal, writing thank-you notes, or by spending some time daily on reflections of gratitude. By incorporating gratitude into your daily routine, you can cultivate a more positive and grateful mindset, which can lead to an elevated self-concept.

So we can see that by practicing gratitude, we can elevate our self-concept by increasing our self-esteem, helping us see ourselves in a more positive light, and cultivating a positive mindset. By incorporating gratitude into our daily routine, we can improve our overall well-being and develop a stronger sense of self-worth and self-acceptance.

Engage In Self-Care

Engaging in self-care activities can have a positive impact on our self-concept. Self-care refers to any activity that we engage in to take care of our physical, emotional, and mental well-being. When we prioritize our self-care, we are sending a message to ourselves that we are valuable and worthy of care, which can boost our self-esteem and self-worth.

Research has shown that engaging in self-care activities can have a positive impact on our mental health. A study published in the Journal of Counseling Psychology found that engaging in self-care activities was associated with lower levels of depression and anxiety (Zahniser & Rupert, 2012). Another study found that self-care practices were associated with increased well-being and resilience (Greene et al., 2018).

Engaging in self-care activities can also help us to feel more connected to ourselves and our needs. When we take time to care for ourselves, we are better able to understand and meet our own needs, which can lead to increased feelings of self-acceptance and self-love.

There are many ways to engage in self-care, such as getting enough sleep, eating nutritious foods, exercising regularly, practicing mindfulness, and engaging in hobbies or activities that we enjoy. By prioritizing self-care, we can improve our overall well-being and develop a stronger sense of self-worth and self-acceptance.

In summary, engaging in self-care activities can elevate our self-concept by boosting our self-esteem and self-worth, helping us to feel more connected to ourselves and our needs, and improving our mental health. By prioritizing self-care, we can develop a greater sense of self-love and acceptance, which can lead to a more positive and confident self-concept.

7 Activities That Elevate Self Concept

Many activities can help elevate our self-concept, boost self-esteem, and promote a positive self-image.

Here are some examples:

Affirmations: Affirmations are positive statements that can help reprogram negative self-talk into positive self-talk. Repeat affirmations daily such as "I am capable of achieving my goals," "I am worthy of love and respect", or "I trust myself to make the right decisions".

Journaling: Writing about our thoughts, feelings, and experiences can help us gain insight into ourselves and our behaviors and promote self-awareness and self-acceptance. Write about your strengths, accomplishments, and the things you are grateful for.

Exercise: Physical activity releases endorphins, which can boost mood and energy levels. Exercise can also promote a sense of accomplishment and boost self-confidence.

Mindfulness: Practicing mindfulness can help us become more aware of our thoughts and feelings and reduce stress and anxiety. Mindfulness techniques include meditation, deep breathing, and body scanning.

Creative expression: Engaging in creative activities such as painting, drawing, or writing can help us express our emotions and boost self-esteem. Don't worry about being perfect, focus on the process and enjoy the activity.

Learning new skills: Learning new skills can help us gain a sense of mastery and accomplishment, and boost self-confidence. Take a class or workshop on something that interests you, or try a new hobby or activity.

Surrounding yourself with positivity: Surround yourself with people who are supportive, positive, and uplifting. Spend time with friends and family who make you feel good about yourself.

By engaging in these activities regularly, we can improve our self-concept, boost self-esteem, and lead a more fulfilling life.

Exercises To Improve Self-Talk

One trick is to think about self-talk like a mental muscle, instead of something abstract. Like all muscles, self-talk takes work and exercise to become strong. Here are three exercises you can use to challenge yourself as you grow your self-talk muscle.

The Listening Challenge

To understand your self-talk, start by keeping a diary and making notes about the frequency of your positive and negative self-talk, the events, people, or situations that trigger it, and the common themes. Reflect on your notes and ask yourself questions like:

- What thoughts come up most often today?
- Why did they come up?
- How can switching to positive self-talk help me achieve my goals?

Finally, think about the accuracy of your self-talk, challenge the assumptions, and look for evidence that goes against your negative beliefs. For instance, if you find yourself thinking "I'm not smart enough to pass this test," challenge it against your past.

Have you succeeded at something you didn't think you would before? How much have you studied? How many years of education have you made it through to get to this point? What are you best at, and what does that say about your potential?

The Spin Challenge

Politicians and other members of the public space often dedicate a specific individual, and sometimes even a team, to spinning negative stories. These people make it a practice of finding the silver lining where others only see storm clouds, thus challenging the narrative, and creating more space for opportunity and success.

When you do the spin challenge, your goal is to identify negative self-talk and replace it with positive self-talk. For instance, instead of saying, "I am such an idiot! I screwed up that project and there's no coming back from that," say "I didn't do as well as I know I can but that's okay. Now I know what I can do next time to be better, and that will help my personal and professional growth." Practice this exercise regularly to develop the habit of positive self-talk.

The Accuracy Challenge

To challenge negative beliefs and switch to positive self-talk, ask questions like where the belief comes from, if the information it's based on is factual, why you believe it, and how accurate it is.

Make a list of situations that go against the negative self-talk statement, such as every time someone thanked you for your help or good work, every time you felt confident about yourself, and every time you've been successful, no matter how small. This exercise will help you create a more realistic and balanced profile of yourself, including both your strengths and areas for improvement.

50 Self-Talk Statements That Elevate Your Self Concept

As we mentioned before, affirmations can be a great tool in elevating your self-concept. But what do affirmations look like? They're phrases, and declarations, which communicate positivity and optimism to ourselves. At first, it may feel odd, but when affirming yourself becomes a habit, you'll begin to see the power that speaking positivity over yourself can have.

Here are 50 statements to start your journey with:

I am capable of achieving my goals.

I am confident in my abilities.

I am deserving of love and respect.

I am a valuable member of my community.

I am grateful for all of my blessings.

I am capable of overcoming any obstacle.

I am worthy of success and happiness.

I am a powerful and resilient individual.

I am proud of myself and my accomplishments.

I am constantly growing and learning.

I am in control of my thoughts and emotions.

I am committed to living a healthy and fulfilling life.

I am positive and optimistic.

I am deserving of forgiveness and second chances.

I am worthy of all the best life has to offer.

I am worthy of achieving my dreams.

I am comfortable in my own skin.

I am able to make a positive impact in the world.

I am able to handle challenges with grace and ease.

I am grateful for my unique qualities and talents.

I am worthy of self-care and self-love.

I am able to overcome fear and take risks.

I am able to forgive myself for past mistakes.

I am deserving of a fulfilling and meaningful life.

I shine bright when I am my most real and genuine self.

I am grateful for the people and experiences in my life.

I am capable of making a difference in the world.

I am able to find peace and happiness within myself.

I am deserving of respect and kindness from others.

I am able to find joy in the present moment.

I am constantly growing and improving as a person.

I am enough just as I am.

I am able to let go of negative thoughts and emotions.

I am worthy of love and affection.

I am capable of achieving my wildest dreams.

I am grateful for the lessons I have learned in life.

I am capable of achieving great success.

I am filled with positive and uplifting energy.

I am able to overcome any challenge that comes my way.

I am deserving of peace and tranquility in my life.

I am able to make positive changes in my life.

I am able to learn from my mistakes and grow from them.

I deserve to grow as a person to become my best possible self.

I am capable of handling any situation with confidence.

I am grateful I take advantage of all the opportunities in my life.

I am able to find meaning and purpose in my life.

I am worthy of self-respect and self-esteem.

I am capable of achieving balance in my life.

I am deserving of a life filled with joy and happiness.

I am able to create the life I desire.

Mental Health Professionals

A trained mental health professional, such as a therapist or counselor, can be irreplaceable in helping individuals improve their self-concept. These professionals have the skills and training to guide individuals through the process of identifying and addressing negative self-talk, challenging distorted thoughts and beliefs, and developing healthy coping mechanisms.

One way a mental health professional can help improve self-concept is by facilitating cognitive behavioral therapy (CBT). CBT is a type of therapy that focuses on changing negative thought patterns and behaviors that are contributing to emotional distress.

Through CBT, individuals can learn how to recognize negative self-talk, challenge it, and replace it with more positive and realistic thoughts. By doing so, individuals can improve their overall self-concept and experience a greater sense of self-worth.

Another way mental health professionals can help improve self-concept is by utilizing other types of therapy, such as mindfulness-based therapy or acceptance and commitment therapy (ACT).

These therapies can help individuals become more aware of their thoughts and emotions and learn how to accept themselves and their experiences with greater compassion and understanding. By practicing self-compassion and self-acceptance, individuals can improve their self-concept and develop a greater sense of self-worth.

In addition to therapy, mental health professionals can also provide guidance and support in developing healthy coping mechanisms. This can include strategies for managing stress, practicing self-care, and engaging in activities that promote mental and emotional well-being. By developing healthy coping mechanisms, individuals can improve their overall self-concept and feel better equipped to handle life's challenges.

Mental health professionals play a critical role in helping individuals improve their self-concept. Through therapy and guidance, individuals can learn how to recognize and challenge negative self-talk, develop healthy coping mechanisms, and cultivate greater self-compassion and self-acceptance. By doing so, individuals can improve their mental and emotional well-being, and experience a greater sense of self-worth and fulfillment in life.

5 Books About Self-Talk

As with most things in life, learning to improve our self-concept is a marathon, not a sprint. There are many great books available that can help you elevate your self-concept and increase your confidence. Here are five highly recommended options:

· *"The Power of Positive Thinking"* by Norman Vincent Peale - This classic book is a great starting point for anyone looking to improve their self-talk and develop a more positive outlook on life.

· *"The Seven Habits of Highly Effective People"* by Stephen Covey - This book is a must-read for anyone interested in personal growth and development. Covey's seven habits provide a roadmap for improving your self-concept and achieving your goals.

· *"The Gifts of Imperfection"* by Brené Brown - In this book, Brown explores the concept of self-acceptance and encourages readers to embrace their imperfections as a means of cultivating self-love and authenticity.

· *"Mindset: The New Psychology of Success"* by Carol S. Dweck - Dweck's book focuses on the power of mindset and how adopting a growth mindset can help individuals develop a more positive self-concept and achieve greater success in their personal and professional lives.

· *"The Art of Possibility"* by Rosamund Stone Zander and Benjamin Zander - This book provides a unique perspective on personal growth and self-concept by encouraging readers to embrace the possibilities of life and approach challenges with a sense of curiosity and creativity.

These books can serve as valuable resources for anyone looking to elevate their self-concept and develop a more positive, confident outlook on life.

5 Ways To Help Others

Helping others has also been shown to help ourselves. Encouraging and supporting others' self-concept can not only have a positive impact on their overall well-being and confidence but in turn, creates genuine connections that can feed into your own life when necessary. With this in mind, here are some practices you can do to help encourage others' self-concept:

Offer genuine praise and recognition - When someone does something well, make sure to acknowledge their accomplishments and offer genuine praise. This can help boost their self-esteem and encourage them to continue working towards their goals.

Provide constructive feedback - While it's important to offer praise, it's also important to provide constructive feedback that can help someone improve. Be sure to offer feedback in a supportive and non-judgmental way, focusing on specific areas where they can improve.

Listen actively and attentively - When someone is sharing their thoughts or feelings with you, make sure to listen actively and attentively. This can help them feel heard and validated, which can increase their confidence and self-esteem.

Celebrate their strengths - Everyone has unique strengths and talents, and it's important to celebrate these qualities in others. Encourage them to pursue activities that align with their strengths and offer support and encouragement along the way.

Be a positive role model - Your behavior and attitude can have a significant impact on others' self-concept. Be a positive role model by practicing self-care, setting healthy boundaries, and maintaining a positive outlook on life.

By incorporating these practices into your interactions with others, you can help encourage and support their self-concept, leading to increased confidence, resilience, and overall well-being.

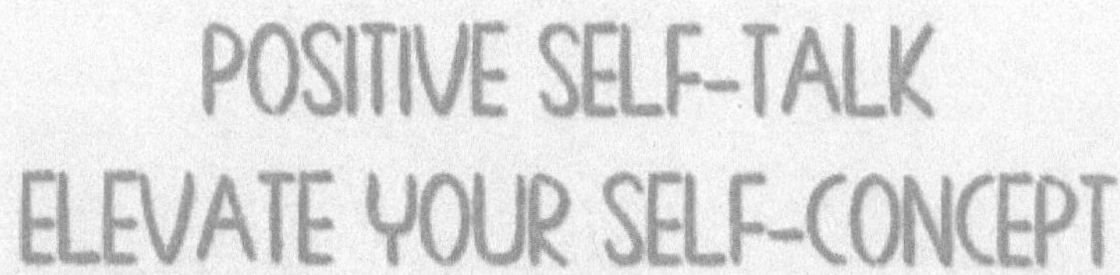
POSITIVE SELF-TALK
ELEVATE YOUR SELF-CONCEPT

I AM CAPABLE OF ACHIEVING MY GOALS.

I AM CONFIDENT IN MY ABILITIES.

I AM DESERVING OF LOVE AND RESPECT.

I AM A VALUABLE MEMBER OF MY COMMUNITY.

I AM GRATEFUL FOR ALL OF MY BLESSINGS.

I AM CAPABLE OF OVERCOMING ANY OBSTACLE.

I AM WORTHY OF SUCCESS AND HAPPINESS.

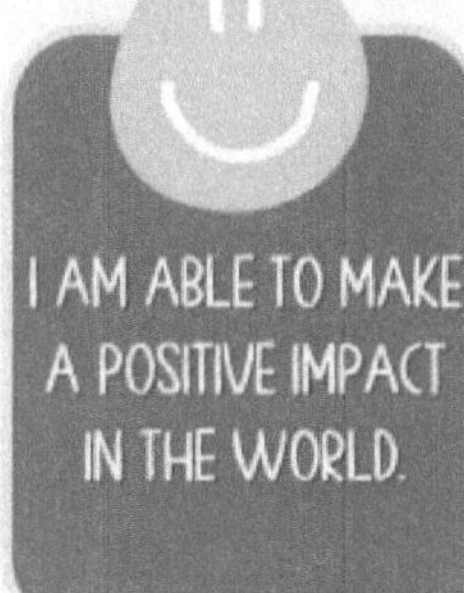

POSITIVE SELF-TALK
ELEVATE YOUR SELF-CONCEPT
I AM WORTHY OF ALL THE BEST LIFE HAS TO OFFER.
I AM WORTHY OF ACHIEVING MY DREAMS.
I AM COMFORTABLE IN MY OWN SKIN.
I AM ABLE TO MAKE A POSITIVE IMPACT IN THE WORLD.
I AM ABLE TO HANDLE CHALLENGES WITH GRACE AND EASE.
I AM GRATEFUL FOR MY UNIQUE QUALITIES AND TALENTS.
I AM WORTHY OF SELF-CARE AND SELF-LOVE.

POSITIVE SELF-TALK
ELEVATE YOUR SELF-CONCEPT

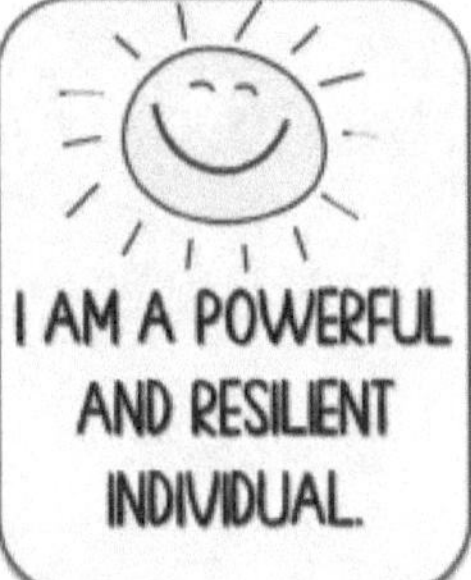

I AM CONSTANTLY GROWING AND LEARNING.

I AM PROUD OF MYSELF AND MY ACCOMPLISHMENTS.

‹‹ Feeling Good About Me ››

I AM IN CONTROL OF MY THOUGHTS AND EMOTIONS.

I AM COMMITTED TO LIVING A HEALTHY AND FULFILLING LIFE.

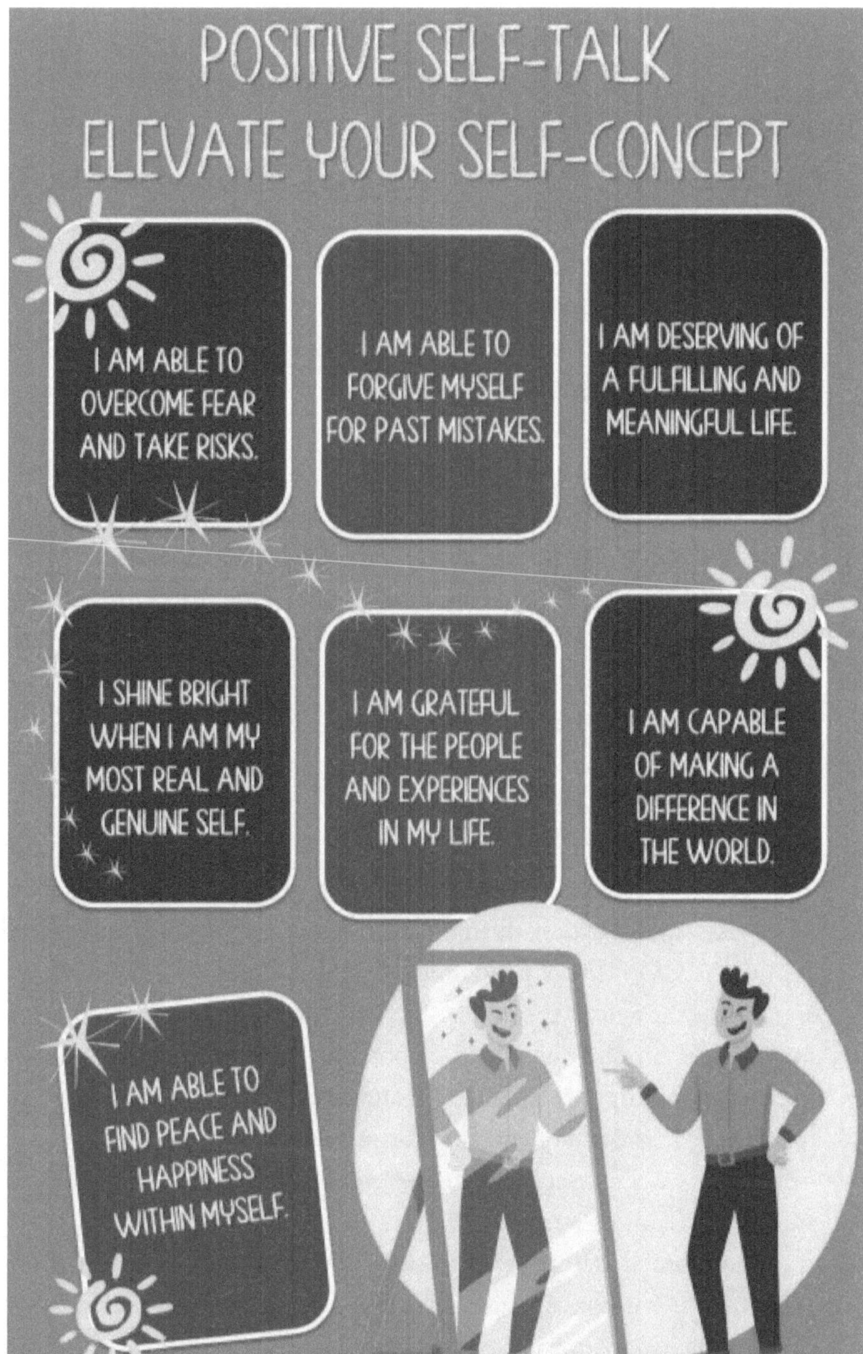
POSITIVE SELF-TALK
ELEVATE YOUR SELF-CONCEPT
I AM ABLE TO OVERCOME FEAR AND TAKE RISKS.
I AM ABLE TO FORGIVE MYSELF FOR PAST MISTAKES.
I AM DESERVING OF A FULFILLING AND MEANINGFUL LIFE.
I SHINE BRIGHT WHEN I AM MY MOST REAL AND GENUINE SELF.
I AM GRATEFUL FOR THE PEOPLE AND EXPERIENCES IN MY LIFE.
I AM CAPABLE OF MAKING A DIFFERENCE IN THE WORLD.
I AM ABLE TO FIND PEACE AND HAPPINESS WITHIN MYSELF.

Final Thoughts

In conclusion, self-talk and self-concept are powerful tools that can have a significant impact on our lives. Positive self-talk can help us build a strong and resilient self-concept, which in turn can benefit our mental health, relationships, work, sports, cognitive performance, health, and creativity. By using positive language to talk to ourselves about our abilities, achievements, and potential, we can cultivate a more optimistic and confident outlook on life.

Research has shown that positive self-talk can lead to increased motivation, persistence, and confidence, which can lead to better outcomes in various domains of our lives. Positive self-talk can also reduce feelings of stress and anxiety, improve immune function, and promote overall well-being. By reinforcing positive beliefs and attitudes about ourselves and the world around us, positive self-talk can help us lead happier, healthier, and more fulfilling lives.

Furthermore, a strong self-concept can serve as a foundation for resilience in the face of adversity. When we have a positive and confident self-concept, we are better able to cope with challenges and setbacks and are more likely to bounce back from adversity. This resilience can be especially important during times of stress and uncertainty, such as during the COVID-19 pandemic.

However, negative self-talk can have harmful consequences for our mental and physical health, relationships, and performance. When we use negative language to talk to ourselves, we are more likely to feel discouraged, anxious, and unmotivated. This can lead to negative outcomes such as depression, anxiety, and decreased performance in various domains of our lives.

Therefore, it is important to be aware of our self-talk and the impact it has on our self-concept and overall well-being. We can practice positive self-talk by using affirmations, focusing on our strengths, and reframing negative thoughts into positive ones. It is also important to seek support from trusted friends, family members, or mental health professionals when negative self-talk affects our mental health and well-being.

References

● Brown, J. D. (2015). Understanding the self. Routledge.

● Harter, S. (2012). The construction of the self: Developmental and sociocultural foundations. Guilford Press.

● Markus, H., & Wurf, E. (1987). The dynamic self-concept: A social psychological perspective. Annual Review of Psychology, 38(1), 299-337.

● Stryker, S., & Burke, P. J. (2000). The past, present, and future of an identity theory. Social Psychology Quarterly,

● Neff, K. D., & McGehee, P. (2010). Self-compassion and psychological resilience among adolescents and young adults. Self and Identity, 9(3), 225-240.

● Wasylkiw, L., MacKinnon, A. L., & MacLellan, A. M. (2012). Exploring the link between self-compassion and body image in university women. Body Image, 9(2), 236-245.

● Leary, M. R., Tate, E. B., Adams, C. E., Batts Allen, A., & Hancock, J. (2007). Self-compassion and reactions to unpleasant self-relevant events: The implications of treating oneself kindly. Journal of Personality and Social Psychology, 92(5), 887-904.

● Locke, E. A., & Latham, G. P. (2002). Building a practically useful theory of goal setting and task motivation: A 35-year odyssey. American Psychologist, 57(9), 705-717.

• Zimmerman, B. J., & Kitsantas, A. (1997). Developmental phases in self-regulation: Shifting from process goals to outcome goals. Journal of Educational Psychology, 89(1), 29-36.

• Heatherton, T. F., & Polivy, J. (1991). Development and validation of a scale for measuring state self-esteem. Journal of Personality and Social Psychology, 60(6), 895–910.

• Vida, M., & Cramer, K. M. (2016). Social support and positive self-concept: The mediating role of identity style. Journal of Adolescence, 47, 155-163.

• Govindji, R., & Linley, P. A. (2007). Strengths use self-concordance and well-being: Implications for strengths coaching and coaching psychologists. International Coaching Psychology Review, 2(2), 143-153.

• Linley, P. A., Nielsen, K. M., Gillett, R., & Biswas-Diener, R. (2010). Using signature strengths in pursuit of goals: Effects on goal progress, need satisfaction, and well-being, and implications for coaching psychologists. International Coaching Psychology Review, 5(1), 6-15.

• Bono, G., Emmons, R. A., & McCullough, M. E. (2010). Gratitude in practice and the practice of gratitude. In Handbook of positive psychology (pp. 553-566). Oxford University Press.

• Toepfer, S. M., Cichy, K., & Peters, P. (2012). Letters of gratitude: Improving well-being through expressive writing. Journal of Writing Research, 4(3), 277-299.

● Greene, T., Cashwell, C. S., & Brinke, J. T. (2018). Self-care practices and resilience: The moderating role of mindfulness. Journal of Counseling & Development, 96(1), 35-45.

● Zahniser, E., & Rupert, P. A. (2012). Relationship of self-care to emotional distress and cortisol secretion in graduate students. Journal of Counseling Psychology, 59(4), 472-478.

| Page

Did you love *The Complete Guide To Positive Self Talk and Your Self Concept*? Then you should read *Master Your Destiny - The Anything Is Possible Mindset*[1] by Danny Nandy!

[2]

Stop and think for a second, what is it that gets you out of bed every morning?

Is it the fact that you have to go to work?

Or is it that every single day you have a new opportunity to make something out of yourself?

What could you achieve if you believed anything is possible? How many doors would open in your life when you adopt the power mindset of "anything is possible?

---

1. https://books2read.com/u/mvyN9q

2. https://books2read.com/u/mvyN9q

It's a natural human tendency to want to pigeonhole ourselves. We like to think that we know who we are, what we're good at, and what we're not good at.

We like to think that we understand our limitations.

But the truth is, we often don't know ourselves nearly as well as we think we do. We self-impose limitations that prevent us from achieving our full potential.

So today, I want to encourage you to break out of your comfort zone and become open to all possibilities. Life is full of surprises - you never know what you might achieve if you just set your mind to it!

Also by Danny Davis

The Complete Guide To Positive Self Talk and Your Self Concept